Between
Promise and fulfillment,
Between
Need and provision
There is
The Waiting Room.

Dear Pat ~ Wonderful to minister with you

Be encouraged! Blessings Await

Keturah Leonforde.

"Waiting Room is an inspiring book about how to wait on God. Keturah's insights are drawn from the experiences of key biblical figures who found themselves in a time of waiting for God's direction. Readers who find themselves in their personal waiting room will be encouraged and will find hope in the pages of this wonderfully written book."

Dr. Lisa M. S. Barrow, D.M.
Founder, Center for Philanthropian Leadership
Author, Hope for a Healthy Workplace

"The Waiting Room has been a tremendous blessing for me as I experience my own time of transition. Leonforde has given practical and spiritual insights into biblical characters and their own waiting room experiences, allowing us to know that we are not alone, forsaken, or forgotten by our great God. You will be blessed and encouraged by this book...praise waits!!!"

Michael Austin, Singer/Songwriter

"Reading this book felt almost like spending a few delightful hours with the author. Her wisdom, humor and compassion always inspire and comfort me, regardless of what is happening in our respective lives when we get together. I am delighted she has decided to share her reflections through this book so she can touch your life with her positive energy as well. Enjoy!"

Wilda B. Graham, Former MBA classmate

reflections from the
WAITING ROOM
Insights for thriving when life puts you on hold

KETURAH LEONFORDE

Essence
PUBLISHING

Belleville, Ontario, Canada

Reflections from the Waiting Room
Copyright © 2006, Keturah Leonforde

All Scripture quotations, unless otherwise specified, are taken from the Holy Bible, *New Living Translation*. (Copyright © 1996. Used by permission of Tyndale House Publishers, Inc., Wheaton, Illinois 60189. All rights reserved.)

Library and Archives Canada Cataloguing in Publication

Leonforde, Keturah, 1966-

   Reflections from the waiting room / Keturah Leonforde.

ISBN 1-55306-975-7

   1. Change (Psychology)—Religious aspects—Christianity. 2. Waiting (Philosophy)—Religious aspects—Christianity. I. Title.

BV4832.3.L46 2005   242'.4   C2005-907069-2

For more information or
to order additional copies, please contact:
thewaitingroom@rogers.com

Essence Publishing is a Christian Book Publisher dedicated to furthering the work of Christ through the written word.
For more information, contact:

20 Hanna Court, Belleville, Ontario, Canada K8P 5J2.
Phone: 1-800-238-6376. Fax: (613) 962-3055.
E-mail: info@essencegroup.com
Web site: www.essencegroup.com/publishing

Printed in Canada
by

Essence
P U B L I S H I N G

Dedication

This book is dedicated to my mother, Lois Harris, who has never hesitated to accompany me to various waiting rooms. She has taught me what it means to wait with patience, with humour, and in service to others—awesome traits to have in any Waiting Room!

Table of Contents

Reflections

Acknowledgements

There is an African proverb that states, "It takes a village to raise a child." Surely it has taken no less than a village to nurture this book from concept to reality.

To all those who have been "village people" in this parenting process, to those who have encouraged, enlightened, and enabled me to persevere to completion—Thank you and God bless!

I especially need to thank:

My siblings, Bev, Al and Michael for envisioning greater things for me than I saw for myself – you continue to give me the courage to be the best I can be – love you guys!

Rob and Elizabeth for encouraging and affirming my voice "for such a time as this". You are a tribute to the coaching community!

Wilda, my soul sister and multi-talented communications guru; There really is a fine line between "better" and "best" and your input helped me to cross it. May God grant you the desires of your heart – my phenomenal friend!

Essence Publishing for believing in me right from the start and patiently sticking with me through this long and dynamic process. Your commitment to inspiring the world through the written word is evident in all you do. May God bless the work of your hands.

My accommodating husband and life partner, Tyron. Without a doubt, your support has literally made this project possible. On behalf of myself and the countless others who will be impacted by these reflections, Eternal love and thanks!

A Note to Prospective Readers

As a seasoned management consultant, I have spent many years managing the expectations of my clients. Consequently, I feel absolutely compelled to provide you with the same courtesy so that you can determine if this volume is worth your while.

Those who know me best will know that I have never claimed to be a Bible scholar. I have never sat through an advanced seminary course, never studied the Bible in its original languages, and never darkened the doorway of a Bible training college (although I did complete my undergrad degree at a Christian university, so that may count for something!) So from a theological-studies standpoint, I am a novice, at best.

From a spiritual standpoint, however, I am surprised and humbled to state that God is doing a new thing in my life. He alone has gifted me with the creative intellect and the active imagination that has resulted in this innovative yet practical set of Waiting-Room reflections. These simple entries are designed for those who have or will take up residence in the Waiting Rooms of life.

I am relieved that God has at least given me a topic with which I am intimately acquainted. Change, transition, disappointment, hope deferred—my life has been characterized by many unexpected, unwelcome, and involuntary forays into the Waiting Room. As a result, when I write to you, I write to myself as well.

So dear reader, I humbly present this book to you, not from an intellectual head space, but from a spirit-led heart place.

If you are in pursuit of deep theological doctrines—this may not be the book for you.

If you have a quest for profound philosophical theories—these may not be the readings for you.

If, however, like me, you have been waiting for thought-provoking, soul-nourishing insights, human-interest stories, and pragmatic tips for enduring those pesky "in-between" times, have I got great news for you. God has sent you a message through me. Your help has arrived. Finally, your wait is over!

Be Blessed,
Keturah

Introduction

In June of 2004, I made the decision to leave my organization, as one of the last in a two-year, 2000-employee, acquisition downsizing. It was not an easy decision for me to make. I enjoyed my status, my work (on most days!), my autonomy and, yes, my regular paycheque! Nevertheless, the time had come for me to step out and explore what I believed was God's fuller purpose for my life. I was very confident—and anticipated great things!

So my journey into new horizons began, and I waited. And waited. And waited a little (and then a lot) longer. I took a trip, redecorated a room, began professional development course work, while I waited, but still nothing remarkable or miraculous happened. My emotions began to waver—anxiety, frustration, impatience, guilt, and fears of incompetence plagued my thoughts. My finances began to dwindle. My health began to suffer. And those around me questioned the wisdom and practicality of my "step-out-in-faith" strategy. I slowly came to the realization that God had ushered me in to life's Waiting Room.

That's when the concept for this survival guide was born. As I began to look beyond my own circumstances, I realized that many people around me were also hanging out in life's Waiting Room. Good people. Spiritual people. Talented people. Committed people. People who shared the common bond of being ushered voluntarily or (more often) involuntarily to this place of waiting, transition, and anticipation—not knowing how or when or even if God was going to move them beyond this place in life.

A funny thing about Waiting Rooms: have you ever really paid attention to how people act in Waiting Rooms? The range of behaviour is as diverse as the individuals themselves. Some make productive use of their time—checking Blackberrys, responding to voice mail, filling out to-do lists. Others distract themselves with outdated magazines or inconsequential small talk. Still others "zone out," simply gazing out into space or catching a snooze, literally waiting for the waiting to be over. One thing is sure, everyone comes to the Waiting Room for a specific purpose—to see someone, to do something—and almost always their objective is achieved; it's just a matter of time. So knowing that waiting has a purpose that will lead to fulfilling specific objectives, doesn't it make sense for us to become really good at waiting?

I have pulled together a few Biblical examples of "waiters" who may teach us a thing or two about hanging out in life's Waiting Room successfully. I hope that whether you are currently in the Waiting Room, about to leave the Waiting Room, or anticipating a Waiting Room in your future, you will wait with purpose, allowing God to fulfill His specific objective for you. Life has shown us that the waiting period will eventually end. Only the lessons learned and qualities developed through the waiting will endure. Hopefully by reviewing these examples from this perspective, you will be able to develop your own game plan for optimizing your stay in life's Waiting Room.

Definition

Wait (wat) v.i. 1. to hold oneself ready for an arrival or occurrence. 2. to be in expectation of something. 3. to be left undone. 4. to serve as a waiter or waitress. (The Random House Dictionary)

Key Reflection Texts

But those who wait on the LORD will find new strength. They will fly high on wings like eagles. They will run and not grow weary. They will walk and not faint (Isaiah 40:31).

Be still in the presence of the LORD, and wait patiently for him to act (Psalm 37:7).

"For I know the plans I have for you," says the LORD. "They are plans for good and not for disaster, to give you a future and a hope" (Jeremiah 29:11).

Your Waiting-Room experience may not be about you!

Noah—120 Years in the Waiting Room

**"So Noah did everything exactly as
God had commanded him."
Genesis 6:22**

suggested reading: Genesis 6,7

Noah was no stranger to the Waiting-Room experience. Can you imagine being called to create something you have never seen (a boat!), for a purpose you have never heard of (flood protection), on behalf of an unsupportive and hostile public with which you have no affiliation—and to keep on doing this every day for 120 years? Ouch! Most of us will go to any length to avoid even a momentary public embarrassment, so just try to imagine what Noah must have gone through, every day, for 43,800 long days. Noah would have gotten up every morning to resume a seemingly ridiculous and apparently futile community project. Luckily for him, it would appear that Noah's self-image was not tied to public approval or deep affiliations. In Genesis 6:9, we read, *"Noah was a righteous man, the only blameless man living on earth at the time."* The word *only* strongly suggests that, within his community and immediate family, Noah was an anomaly. In fact, it is likely that Noah's "right doing" and single-minded determination to follow God's will ultimately saved the lives of his family. After all, there is no mention of *their* righteousness! In Genesis 7:1, God reiterates, *"Go into the boat with all your family...I consider you alone to be righteous."*

The wonderful thing we learn about Noah as we review his 120-year Waiting-Room experience is that, despite the scientific odds (it had never rained before!) and lack of public approval, Noah made an important choice. In Genesis we are told, *"He consistently followed God's will and [consequently] enjoyed a close relationship with Him...Noah did everything exactly as God had commanded him"* (Genesis 6:9,22). So while Noah seemed to be somewhat lacking in the popularity department, he chose the one affiliation that mattered most— a personal, committed relationship to God. While Noah did not seem to have had many friends, he did have one important friend. And if you can only have one friend, that friend needs to be God, who will instruct you and encourage you through the Waiting-Room experiences of life.

There is something else that we learn from Noah's 120-year Waiting-Room experience. Noah's 120-year wait was society's 120-year chance—an opportunity for individuals to follow Noah's pleading, turn to God, and be saved. Your Waiting-Room experience may not be about you! It may be that God is working on the hearts and souls of others and your wait is designed to save and transform *their* lives. Noah was probably spiritually ready to jump into the boat when God first gave the command to build. The same God, who in Genesis 1 had created an entire Earth system in seven days, certainly did not need an additional 43,793 days of man's time to build a single boat! But God was allowing society an opportunity to come to its senses! God's redeeming love was being demonstrated through His perseverance with man, and He used Noah to graphically and orally communicate that message to the world for a period of 120 mercifully long years.

Real-Time Reflection

Today you may find yourself in a seemingly permanent Waiting-Room situation. Perhaps God has asked you to create or pursue something that seems ridiculous or futile and may even be the source of humiliation and public embarrassment. Noah's example of obedience and commitment to his strange, long-term assignment models God's desire for you today. By forming a close and personal affiliation with God, you will be strengthened and encouraged in your commitment to persevere through your own Waiting-Room assignment. Keep in mind too that, like Noah, your Waiting-Room experience may not even be about you! Perhaps God in His wisdom and mercy is using your experience to spark transformation in the lives of others. Ultimately, only eternity will reveal the true purpose of some of our Waiting-Room situations. However, with examples like Noah's available to us today, surely that future revelation will be worth the wait!

Although God's timing
might be different than
our human understanding,
it is always right.

Noah Waits—Again

**"But God remembered Noah and
all the animals in the boat."
Genesis 8:1**

suggested reading: Genesis 8

It's a good thing that Noah was intimately familiar with the Waiting Room, because God had him visit it on at least one more occasion during his life. For an entire week, Noah and his family waited in the ark for an unprecedented rainfall to occur. To heighten the drama of this scene, Bible scholars estimate that there were approximately 45,000 animals that participated in this strange family gathering. Think of the smells, think of the cabin fever, think of the doubts and questions that must have been hurled at Noah as his family sat cooped up in this ridiculous-looking structure, while crowds jeered day and night from the outside. At least during the previous 120 years of waiting, Noah and his family had been free to come and go from the contentious scene of the ark. Those final seven days of waiting on board the ship must have felt like an eternity to Noah and his family.

At last, after a week of claustrophobic anticipation, the promised rain fell and fell and fell some more. Noah appeared to be vindicated, at last! God had fulfilled His promise, at last! The jeering stopped and an entire evil nation was wiped out, at last! The ark of ridicule had become an ark of refuge, and for some reason, even the animals didn't smell so bad anymore! For forty days and nights, praise and worship services ascended from the inner sanctuary. For forty days, while the showers poured, all was well.

But then the rain stopped. Note the timeline: 150 days later, the boat finally rested on Mount Ararat; seventy-five days later, other mountain peaks appeared; forty days after that, a raven was released from the boat; then a dove was released and returned; seven days later, the dove was released again; seven days after that, the dove was released for the last time. In total, almost twelve months passed between the time Noah and his family first stepped into the boat and the time God said to Noah, *"Leave the boat, all of you"* (Genesis 8:16). Now, I imagine the initial forty days and nights of rainfall activity were great days to appreciate being on the boat. But to stay on for months and months after the rain had stopped? Let's just say my praise would have worn thin and my worship would have been more hollow than holy! Although Noah repeatedly conducted the scientific "bird test" to determine the dryness of the elements, even after the results appeared positive, he did not leave the boat until God commanded it. Noah understood that the Creator knew better than the created one when the elements would be most suitable for human re-habitation. Noah understood that although God's timing might be different than our human understanding, it is always right. We are assured that *"God remembered Noah and all the animals in the boat"* (Genesis 8:1) even through that long year when they might have felt abandoned, frustrated, and as if that was how they would be spending the remainder of their "stinking" lives.

Real-Time Reflection

Have you ever felt left out, left behind, or just plain left over? Are there times in the Waiting-Room experiences of your life when you have felt abandoned, forgotten, or even cursed to a "stinking" existence by God? I have! Together, let's find comfort in the fact that the same God who remembered Noah and all the animals in the boat will remember us during our Waiting-Room experiences. Let's keep the praise and worship going beyond the obvious "showers-of-blessing" days, confident that God—our Creator—will safely guide us—His created ones—to the most suitable elements and situations for our lives.

God's delay is never an invitation
to formulate and implement a
do-it-yourself plan.

Abram: Also the Father of Many

**"O Sovereign LORD, what good
are all your blessings when I
don't even have a son?"
Genesis 15:2**

suggested reading: Genesis 12-25

The story of Abram is a classic tale of life in the Waiting Room. As God called Abram out of Haran to re-settle in Canaan, He pronounced a holistic blessing like no other on Abram. Abram was assured that he was going to be outrageously blessed—personally, materially, and publicly (see Genesis 12:2). Let's face it, as far as blessings go, this proclamation was about as good as it gets! I imagine that Abram was quite thrilled and full of confidence with God's declaration at first. Abram, and his wife Sarai, already owned significant wealth (12:5), they were en route to a promising new region (11:31) and, at the age of seventy-five, Abram was still somewhat in the running to become a father. After all, his own father, Terah, was in *his* seventies when he had Abram (11:26).

But a strange thing happens when we think we have had to wait a little too long for what is rightfully ours. In our Waiting-Room situation, we tend to get very short-sighted. We can't seem to see beyond what we lack to simply enjoy what we already have. Although Abram acknowledged that he had indeed been blessed and that God alone was supreme, he discounted all the other demonstrations of ful- filled promises and focused on the one aspect that hadn't yet materialized in his life—namely, children. We will never know for sure why God took His time in fulfilling that part of His promise to Abram. Likely Abram and Sarai's charac- ters were still under construction. Evidently there were still some foundations of faith that needed to be reinforced (see Genesis 12:10-20). Regardless of God's reasons, we need to recognize that "God's delays are not God's denial."[1] Time in the Waiting Room has its purpose. God had not aban- doned Abram. Throughout the years of waiting, Abram had direct and repeated promises from God that a son would eventually come. Furthermore, in case Abram doubted the source of his offspring, God emphasized *"Sarah, your wife, will bear you a son"* (Genesis 17:19).

If Abram and Sarai had continued in obedience, the only real test that Abram and Sarai would have faced was the test of time. All that stood between that couple and the fulfill- ment of that aspect of God's promise was twenty-five addi- tional years and menopause—which really meant very little to the sovereign Lord of the possible. But this couple decided to lend God a helping hand and, consequently, were forced to face a battery of tests. Their actions in orchestrating a sur- rogate pregnancy simultaneously provided evidence of their faith—that the promise would and should be fulfilled—and evidence of their doubt—that the Creator could fulfill it without their assistance. One thing becomes very clear

---

[1] George-Louis Leclec de Baffon (1707-1788) French Naturalist.

through the example of Abram and Sarai: God's delay is never an invitation to formulate and implement a do-it-yourself plan. The consequences of Abram and Sarai's actions were immediate and far-reaching. The familial peace that Abram desired and valued so much was lost, forever. (See Genesis 13:8 to understand the extremes to which Abram went to have peace with his nephew Lot.) An unparalleled legacy of conflict and strife became the defining trademark between Abram's rival descendants, Isaac and Ishmael. So while *Abraham* eventually became the father of many through his son of promise, Isaac, *Abram* also became the father of many through his son of *com*promise, Ishmael.

Real-Time Reflection

Today, while we linger in the Waiting Room, we face the same choices that Abram and Sarai faced. Every day, we can make the choice to stand on God's promises or lean on our *com*promises. We can choose to claim God's promise for *"a future and a hope"* (Jeremiah 29:11), or we can formulate our own plans for living our best lives, right now. We can decide to give birth to faith and the peace that passes all understanding (Philippians 4:7), or we can give birth to doubt with its umbilical cord of fear. Either way, our Waiting-Room experience will ultimately give birth to something.

I'm glad Abram and Sarai finally matured into Abraham and Sarah. I'm relieved their story does not end with Ishmael's birth and that Isaac eventually shows up. It gives me hope that even if I have not exercised as much faith, obedience, and trust in past Waiting-Room experiences, I have the opportunity to turn things around from this moment on, through obedience, dependence, and surrender to God. I want to really experience, like Abraham and Sarah eventually did, the full blessings and laughter that come from watching God work things out *His* way—preferably without having to also contend with the consequences of my own compromises.

Lord, teach me how to surrender and trust in you. Help me to avoid the urge to take matters into my own hands, even while I wait.

Interlude

Tis so sweet to trust in Jesus
Just to take Him at His word
Just to rest upon His promise.
Just to know, "Thus saith the Lord"
Jesus, Jesus how I trust Him
How I've proved Him o'er and o'er
Jesus, Jesus, Precious Jesus
Oh for grace, to trust Him more.

Doing wrong things to achieve right outcomes is not an acceptable way to escape our Waiting Room.

Rebekah: The Trouble with Do-It-Yourself Exit Strategies

**And the LORD told her, "The sons in your
womb will become two rival nations.
One nation will be stronger than the other;
the descendants of your older son will serve
the descendants of your younger son."
Genesis 25:23**

suggested reading: Genesis 25-50

I have yet to figure out what rock Rebekah was living under when she cooked up Jacob's birthright scheme. Perhaps she missed the news flash: "Do-it-yourself strategies don't work!"—even though she had probably heard the story of her in-laws' (Abraham and Sarah) disastrous attempts at surrogate parenthood. Maybe she was oblivious to the resulting family feud between her husband, Isaac, and his half brother, Ishmael, even though there were signs of it all around her. For some strange reason, the message that God does not need human assistance to fulfill His promises had not penetrated Rebekah's psyche.

During pregnancy, the previously barren Rebekah had gotten the word from God himself that her older son would serve her younger son (see Genesis 26:23). God really couldn't have been more explicit than that. Yet somehow God's promise was not good enough for our dear Rebekah. Over time, she grew impatient with her Waiting-Room situation! Over time, she felt that she needed to assist God in facilitating the promised outcome. It is amazing the elaborate lengths Rebekah chose to go to in manipulating the birthright ceremony. Talk about a drama queen! Rebekah made animal-skin gloves, a furry necklace, savoury stew, and even baked fresh bread to execute her convoluted scheme. Clearly Rebekah had lots of spare time on her hands, because each of these preparations would have taken some time to complete.

Speaking of time—imagine if Rebekah had used her Waiting-Room time differently. Imagine if she had poured her energy into seeking God rather than strategizing deceit. Think of what a difference that would have made to her relationship to her son, her husband, and even with herself. Unfortunately, the repercussions of Rebekah's fraudulent actions had both short- and long-term consequences:

- Rebekah never saw her beloved son Jacob again.

- The rift between her sons became deadly, and the family was torn apart by hatred.

- Esau became the founder of an enemy nation.

- Jacob experienced deceit from his uncle Laban.

- Finally, I'm guessing here, the remainder of the marriage between Rebekah and Isaac was less than trusting and tranquil.

Rebekah's life teaches us about the trouble with accelerating our departure from the Waiting Room using do-it-yourself strategies. Like that of her mother-in-law before her, Rebekah's "help" quickly became a "hindrance" to God's master plan, and things really fell apart. If Rebekah had done nothing, Jacob would still have received the birthright. God Himself had promised it. Doing wrong things to achieve right outcomes is not an acceptable way to escape our Waiting Room.

Real-Time Reflection

Are you so tired of your waiting that you are contemplating doing some less-than-great things just to get to the "right outcomes? Are you strategizing complicated plans to accelerate your Waiting-Room departure? Reflect for a moment on Rebekah's experience. Determine whether or not you really are prepared to deal with the full consequences of your actions. I know that waiting is hard. I know that the in-between time can seem dull and endless. But God has promised each of us a future and a hope and, unlike us, He does not deceive and He cannot lie. Keep praising, keep serving, and keep doing the right things—God's deliverance and His outcomes are well worth waiting for!

Our Waiting Room may place us at all-time lows so that God can prepare us for all-time highs.

Joseph: Attitudes and Altitudes

**"Pride goes before destruction,
and haughtiness before a fall."
Proverbs 16:18**

suggested reading: Genesis 37-50

There is a word for the young Joseph we are introduced to in Genesis 37—*brat!* That's the conclusion I arrive at when I study his interactions with his half-brothers. As the obvious favourite of his aging father, Jacob, Joseph enjoyed an openly privileged status. Jacob made no attempt to hide his skewed affection for this son and, as a result, the seed for jealousy and sibling rivalry was planted. Still, without the right conditions, a seed will not grow. Unfortunately, as a spoiled and insensitive younger brother, Joseph became a one-man irrigation system.

Of all the things Joseph did wrong, strutting around in the flashy coat his father gave him was probably the least. Although his father was wrong in singling him out by giving him that special gift, I probably would have worn it too— clearly it was a coat to die for! Where I do blame Joseph, however, is in the obnoxious way in which he inappropriately flaunted his close relationship to his father, his future exalted status, and his prophetic (and pathetic!) dream-

42

interpretation capabilities in front of his brothers. When Joseph experienced a series of dreams that pointed to his future leadership status over his brothers, he did not hesitate to throw this revelation in their faces. Not once but twice, Joseph flaunted his future glory before his brothers, causing the already existing rift between himself and his siblings to widen to a deep chasm. Nothing in Genesis 37 suggests that Joseph approached his brothers for their assistance in interpreting his dreams, for their insights on preparing for his future position, or in a spirit of praise and gratitude to a sovereign God. Everything about the chapter suggests that Joseph was displaying the classic traits of a spoiled brat: tactlessness, arrogance, and immaturity. Those were the very traits that Joseph would need to lose if he were ever to see the fulfillment of those very dreams. While old man Jacob needed a crash course in Equitable Parenting 101, Joseph needed a remedial course in The School of Hard Knocks. As a result, Joseph's Waiting-Room experience would become his personal training college.

A funny thing about attitudes—they tend to alter with altitudes. It is likely that after Joseph's brothers grabbed his precious coat and threw him into a pit to die, Joseph had some moments to reflect on his earlier interactions with his brothers. He probably was focused a little less on his lofty dreams and a little more on his lowly—and possibly deadly—situation. Once he had been literally knocked down to earth, his attitude began to change. We may never know the exact thought processes that Joseph went through, but one thing is clear. By the time he was purchased and became a slave on Potiphar's staff, we are told *"The LORD was with Joseph and blessed him greatly as he served"* (Genesis 39:2). I believe that Joseph's moments in the pit became his path to an authentic relationship with his Heavenly Father. In Proverbs, Solomon warns us clearly that, *"Pride goes before destruction, and haughtiness before a fall"* (Proverbs 16:18). So the fact that, throughout the remainder of Joseph's life, whether as a prisoner or a prime minister, *"The LORD was with him, making everything run smoothly and successfully"* (Genesis 39:23) provides evidence that a remarkable transformation had taken place with Joseph's attitude. We do not know precisely how long Joseph was confined to the pit before being sold to Potiphar. What we do know is that the moments spent were "quality" time. Gone forever is the tattle-telling, tactless, smug, self-sufficient brat we first met. Remarkably, a focused, mature, composed, socially and spiritually savvy young man has emerged from the pit. Joseph is careful to give God the glory in all his achievements and through all his circumstances. The rest of the story is, indeed, *his*tory. Joseph went from being his earthly father's favourite son to his Heavenly Father's favoured one. As a result, he was able to save himself, his family, and ultimately an entire nation from certain death and devastation.

Joseph's life demonstrates that there are no limits to the heights that God's favoured ones can reach, when they possess the right attitudes. We need to recognize that our Waiting Room may place us at all-time lows so that God can prepare us for all-time highs. Imagine, Joseph the seasoned and previously arrogant dreamer, the one who had been interpreting his own dreams since childhood, as a transformed adult responding to Pharaoh's plea for dream interpretation by saying, *"It is beyond my power to do this...But God will tell you what it means"* (Genesis 41:16).

Real-Time Reflection

As you endure a Waiting-Room situation today, do you find yourself in need of an attitude makeover? Are there some maturing, humbling, transformational character changes that are needed in your life? There is no time like the present to begin to work on the necessary adjustments that will prepare you to fulfill God's purpose for your life. Today's lows may well be designed to transform you to appropriately navigate tomorrow's highs.

I am thankful for the example and raw truths of Joseph's early life. They provide me with a sense of confidence as I face a future that is uncertain in its circumstance but certain in its ultimate outcome. God is still in the "extreme makeover" business. My Waiting Room may well be His operating theatre as He prepares me for my "reveal." One thing I am sure about—if I could ask Joseph, he would assure me that God's "reveal" is worth waiting for!

While you are waiting,
God may be shaping
your deliverance.

Moses: A Crisis in Confidence

**"Now Moses was more humble than
any other person on earth."
Numbers 12:3**

suggested reading: Exodus 1-12

I have always found this declaration to be somewhat surprising. Of all the attributes required for successful leadership, humility does not tend to top contemporary lists. Particularly when we consider Moses' background, if any man had reason for pride, it was him. Hand-picked and raised by Pharaoh's daughter, educated in the finest schools of academic and military training, resident of the nation's royal palace—if not born with a silver spoon, Moses certainly seemed to have access to one. Yet Moses never lost sight of who he was on the inside. Though outwardly displaying all the trappings of privilege, Moses remained quietly connected to his people. In fact, as he witnessed the cruelty that the Egyptians showed toward the Israelite slaves day after gruelling day, Moses' anger simmered. It really was only a matter of time before his military training caught up with his anger. Finally, he recklessly murdered a slave-driving Egyptian.

As a result of this seemingly rash behaviour, Moses had to flee for his life. Gone were the status symbols, titles, and social circles to which he had become accustomed as the adopted son of royalty. Gone too were his networks and affiliations among his own Israelite community. Moses became an enemy of the state and a fugitive, forced to live in relative obscurity for forty long years. The oppression and misery of the Israelite slaves continued without an end in sight. But while the Israelites were waiting for deliverance, God was busy shaping their deliverer. Relegated to the role of a common shepherd, Moses was developing the remaining leadership skills that he would need to deal with the children of Israel. The key lesson that higher education and military training had failed to teach Moses was total dependence on God. Killing the Egyptian in the heat of the moment was evidence of Moses' self-reliance. To lead the Israelite multitudes, Moses would need reliance on the Divine. Also, as a Midianite shepherd, Moses was able to truly understand the culture of the Israelites. Prior to his involuntary exile, Moses had deep *sympathy* for the Israelites. By living as a low-class shepherd, on the bottom rung of the socio-economic ladder, Moses developed deep *empathy* for the Israelites. God in His wisdom knew that Moses would need a great deal of empathy to lead a displaced nation of three million fickle, disobedient, ungrateful, faithless, confrontational, rebellious, and disloyal people on a forty-year camping trip!

So for forty years, God shaped the character of Moses. The longer Israel waited, the more God shaped. When God finally came to usher Moses out of his Waiting Room, there was clear evidence that a change had taken place. Exodus 3 and 4 are filled with the protests and excuses that Moses presented to God regarding his leadership appointment. Gone was the cocky, self-reliant, brash youth who killed without thought of consequence. In his place knelt a mature, composed, and, most importantly, humble individual. Life as a shepherd had resulted in Moses trading independence for divine-dependence, rash thinking for rational thinking, and cheekiness for meekness. Finally, Moses was ready to be used by God!

In spite of his extensive Waiting-Room experience, Moses didn't always get it right. I believe the Israelites would have tested the leadership skills of even the most saintly man or woman, particularly for forty seemingly endless years. Ultimately, Moses had a setback, acted in self-reliant anger, and missed out on eligibility for Canaan. Thankfully, the story doesn't end there, and Moses' status in the "Honour Roll of Faith" in Hebrews 11 reassures us that he did not miss out on eligibility for his Heavenly home.

Real-Time Reflection

Where do you find yourself today? Are you stuck in a Waiting-Room period in your own life? Have you waited in vain for that better job, improved relationship, grateful child, more authentic church community? Does it feel as if God has forgotten you and that your change will never come? Learn from the story of Moses that while you are waiting, God may be shaping your deliverance. Cooperate with God to eradicate those character flaws that may be keeping you from your next assignment. Then, when God invites you into your destiny, you can step out mature, surrendered, humble, and ready to be used by Him.

Though the circumstance of
our waiting may be an ordeal,
God's reward for the faithful
will be ideal.

Caleb: Waiting in Vain?

**"But my servant Caleb is
different from the others."
Numbers 14:24**

suggested reading: Numbers 13,14; Joshua 14,15

The story of Caleb inspires me. After all, Caleb was an encourager and an optimist. Caleb was brave and full of faith in God. Caleb viewed life from a divine perspective. So when Caleb returned with the other Israelite scouts from checking out Canaan, the land flowing with milk, honey, and abundant fruit, Caleb brought back a great report. Unfortunately, it was also the minority report. While the other scouts were focused on the insurmountable obstacles, Caleb was focused on his undefeatable God. While the other scouts talked about the size and power of the enemy, Caleb reminded the people of the size and power of their God. And while the other scouts emphasized their military weakness and grasshopper-like status, Caleb attempted to remind the Israelites of God's strength and omnipotent status. It is a sad, sad fact that Caleb and Joshua's optimism stood alone in overwhelming opposition to the negativity of over three million Israelites. In fact, Caleb's faith-filled, optimistic, divinely inspired account fuelled the contempt of the multitude to such an extent that *"the whole community began to talk about stoning Joshua and Caleb"* (Numbers 14:10).

Here's where the story begins to get really strange. As Numbers 14 continues, after some awesome negotiations, Moses was able to persuade God not to instantly wipe out the entire Israelite nation for their lack of faith. God agreed to pardon the Israelites but condemned the entire adult generation to a death sentence—without inheriting the land of promise—due to their lack of faith in God and evil contempt for Joshua and Caleb. There was one notable exception:

> *But my servant Caleb is different from the others. He has remained loyal to me, and I will bring him into the land that he explored. His descendants will receive their full share of the land* (Numbers 14:24).

Although that appeared on the surface to be great news, was it really? Guess who had to hang out with the miserable, contemptuous, pessimistic, faithless mob for another forty years? Caleb. Guess who had to live, work, and worship side by side with the very people who wanted to see him dead for his optimistic attitude? Caleb. Guess who had to go through all the funerals and periods of mourning that would accompany the untimely death of an entire generation of his peers? Caleb. And guess who had to experience all the disease and diminished capacities that are a natural part of a four-decade aging process? Not Caleb!

God rewarded Caleb's faith. In Joshua 14, we see the fulfillment of God's promise to Caleb. Forty-five years after the promise was given, at the age of eighty-five, we have evidence that the miraculous has occurred. We find faith-filled Caleb amazingly fit, fabulous, and ready to fight—exactly as he was when he first scouted out the land of Canaan with

Joshua so many years before. God was good. Caleb waited, but he did not wait in vain. He was rewarded with vitality, health, blessings, and a lasting inheritance *"because he wholeheartedly followed the LORD"* (Joshua 14:14). As a result of his obedient waiting, Caleb's reward transcended time, generations, and expectations. Caleb lived to become an awesome testimony of God's miraculous power and ability to reward His faithful ones.

Real-Time Reflection

As you examine your own Waiting-Room situation, are there elements of your circumstances that are uncomfortable, hostile, and perhaps even toxic? Are there individuals who are testing your faith, tormenting your soul, or taunting your convictions?

From Caleb we can learn the power of positive thinking, viewing obstacles through a divine perspective, and following God with a whole heart. Though the circumstance of our waiting may be an ordeal, God's reward for the faithful will be ideal. Like Caleb, God promises us that our reward will transcend time, generations, and expectations. *"No eye has seen, no ear has heard, and no mind has imagined what God has prepared for those who love him"* (1 Corinthians 2:9). Finally—a reward worth waiting for!

Our best choices will sometimes
involve waiting contentedly on God's
leading, anticipating His deliverance,
and celebrating His restoration
in our lives.

Ruth: Waiting to Celebrate

**"For he is the son of your
daughter-in-law who loves you
so much and who has been better
to you than seven sons!" Ruth 4:15**

suggested reading: Ruth 1-4

I believe we will never fully grasp the essence of Ruth. Many commentators reflect on Ruth's courage, tenacity, and self-sacrificing disposition. Ruth has been heralded through the centuries for her work ethic, integrity, and remarkable benevolence. But there is a more essential quality that I have come to admire as I study the life of Ruth. It would appear that Ruth had mastered the art of contentedly waiting on God's timing, plan, and purpose for her life. Now it is critical that we distinguish between contentment and mediocrity. We don't have to look any further than Ruth's sister-in-law Orpah to see the difference between the two.

Orpah was a character with whom most of us can identify. She appeared to have been a good wife and a good daughter-in-law and in the end she made a "good" choice. Facing a probable future of widowhood, alienation in a foreign culture, poverty, and childlessness, Orpah's decision to follow her mother-in-law's advice and go back to her own people was a sound one. She would return to a familiar culture, lifestyle, religion and, we can assume, a familiar and predictable destiny. She would return to normality and likely she would live happily-ever-after, like so many women of her time. Not only was this Orpah's right according to societal law, it was also a very good decision.

Ruth, however, did not make a "good" decision. Facing a future that would likely involve poverty, low socio-economic status, loneliness, and, ultimately, obscurity, Ruth defied Naomi's request to abandon her and insisted that she would rather risk her normal and predictable future to adopt Naomi's God, people, culture, and land. From every human perspective, it was not a "good" decision. Very few of us would make Ruth's choice or encourage someone close to us to make a decision like the one Ruth made. But after more than a decade with Naomi and her family, in spite of losing a husband, childlessness, and the prospect of a shame-filled, impoverished future, Ruth seemed to have found something that returning to her former lifestyle would not give her. Through Naomi's faith and Naomi's God, Ruth had found contentment. Contentment that was not dependent on financial security, marital status, the stigma of questionable fertility, or the fluctuating emotions of a jaded mother-in-law. That's what I find so remarkable about Ruth's Waiting-Room experience. While Orpah was busy exercising her rights, Ruth got busy exercising her faith. While Orpah willingly choose to return to normality and her comfort zone, Ruth embraced uncertainty and the adventure of the unknown. As Orpah headed down the well-worn path to mediocrity, Ruth voluntarily stepped into the Waiting Room wrapped in the conviction and contentment of her faith and very little else. To further challenge Ruth's decision making, there may have been some concern for Naomi's mental stability. Naomi, whose name means *pleasant*, was in the middle of experiencing her own meltdown and was publicly requesting that her name to be changed to *Mara*, meaning *bitter*; such was the impact of the grief, loss, and deprivation of the previous years. In light of that situation, Ruth's decision to stay with Naomi and care for her was particularly remarkable.

Let's examine another aspect of Ruth's contented disposition. According to Ruth 1, Ruth was married to Naomi's son for approximately ten years, but there were no children born to that marriage. Although there is still some stigma in our society related to childlessness within a marriage, our attitudes absolutely pale in comparison to the obsession that women had in Bible times related to fertility and fruitfulness. Childlessness was seen as a public curse from God, and throughout the Bible, we see women who made delayed pregnancy their platform for prayer, pity, and praise. One need only look at Sarah, Rachel, Hannah, or Elizabeth to see the disgracefulness of a childless condition and the relief that having a child brought (see Luke 1:25). The strange thing with Ruth, however, is that despite her childless condition, at no point do we see her complaining, bargaining, petitioning, or attempting to improve her fertility prospects. Ruth was focused on nurturing what she *did* have, namely her faith and her family (Naomi); her future she left to God. Ruth's willingness to choose the Waiting Room, despite the uncertain prospects of the road ahead, demonstrate that she had learned to measure her value and her security through the eyes of God, not man. By voluntarily choosing to wait on the Lord and anticipate His leading, Ruth was ultimately able to celebrate the restoration of more than she had ever asked for or dared to imagine.

We later learn that through her assertiveness, diligence, and obedience Ruth became not only a mother of a child (Obed) but the grandmother of a king (David) and ultimately a matriarch of the lineage of the Messiah (Jesus). So while Ruth did not make a "good" decision, ultimately she made the "best" decision—the decision to contentedly wait on God's timing and purpose for her life.

Real-Time Reflection

What decisions are you grappling with today? Are you at the crossroads of a decision between good and best? Is there a Waiting-Room situation ahead of you that you need to voluntarily step into? Ruth's example reminds us that our best choices will sometimes involve waiting contentedly on God's leading, anticipating His deliverance, and celebrating His restoration in our lives.

Each day, we face choices between good and best, between mediocrity and excellence, between the ordinary and the extraordinary. Let's pray for Ruth's spirit of contentment, even while we wait and anticipate. The celebration of God's restoration will be well worth waiting for!

Often we must demonstrate a
change in our attitude in order for
God to facilitate a change in
our circumstance.

Hannah: Throwing Away Your Whine

**"Seeing her lips moving but hearing
no sound, he (Eli) thought she had been
drinking. 'Must you come here drunk?'
he demanded. 'Throw away your wine!'"
1 Samuel 1:13,14**

suggested reading: 1 Samuel 1,2

There is a well-known saying that states, "Hell hath no
fury like a woman scorned!" Probably throughout history,
each generation and culture has had its own way of phrasing
this edict. Regardless of the terminology used, the underlying
message is clear: there is very little hope of reasoning with a
woman who has been on the receiving end of contempt or
rejection. Such was the unfortunate lot of Hannah. In spite
of being the object of her husband's attention and affection,
Hannah was in a state of despair. It was bad enough that
after years of marriage to her beloved she had been unable
to produce even one child as evidence of their union. That
"failure" in itself was and continues to be a place of private
pain for women throughout history. But beyond the blight of
infertility, Hannah had to share her husband with the mean-
spirited, arrogant, "in-your-face" Peninnah, who found the
greatest pleasure in reminding Hannah constantly about her
apparent physical, spiritual, and feminine failure. In a time
when barrenness was attributed to the withdrawal of God's

blessing on a woman's life, Peninnah's voice became a constant soul-piercing, conscious-tormenting chord of turmoil in Hannah's daily life.

As a result of Peninnah's taunting and the inner haunting that plagued Hannah's circumstance, I believe Hannah did in fact become drunk. Not drunk through abuse of alcoholic wine—as the high priest Eli deduced when he saw her wordlessly pouring out her heart in the temple—but drunk with the effects of the whine of emotional abuse to which she had been consistently subjected. Make no mistake; when we are placed under severe physical or emotional strain—real or perceived—one of our most innate human responses is to strike up a whine. Hannah was no exception. 1 Samuel describes a scorned woman suffocating in a fury of deep mental anguish, sorrow, bitterness, and profound sadness. Not even the unconditional love of her husband could penetrate Hannah's disillusionment with her lot. Her Waiting-Room circumstance had warped all perspective; sound reasoning now appeared like foolishness in her tear-filled eyes.

God used Eli's sharp words as a wake-up call to Hannah. No doubt Eli, as a long-serving priest for his community, was aware of the situation Hannah was battling. Beyond the situation, he probably knew enough about Hannah's character that the prospect of her arriving at the temple drunk was an unlikely one at best. But by accusing Hannah of drunkenness, Eli was pointing out just how unacceptable her behaviour and attitude had become—in the eyes of man and in the eyes of God. God was testing her in the Waiting Room, and up until this point she was failing her test. Although year after year, Hannah's family had honoured their religious customs and offered ceremonial sacrifices, the sacrifice that God desired from Hannah was the sacrifice of praise, right in the midst of her despicable circumstance. Eli's command *"Throw away your wine!"* cleared Hannah's mind in a way that her husband's love and reassurances had failed to do. Hannah's response (1 Samuel 1:15) demonstrated an immediate clarity of perception, sobriety of thinking, and a recognition of her sinfulness. It is as if Hannah came to herself and, more importantly, cast her cares to God, fully surrendering her circumstance. Hannah literally and symbolically "threw away her whine," and it was in that moment of her sobriety that God, through Eli, was able to hear and honour Hannah's request, encourage her spirit, and begin to pour blessings into her life.

How do we know that Hannah had changed? In response to Eli's pronouncement, we see immediate signs of transformation in Hannah. Hannah replaced her cries of anguish with words of gratitude; her irresponsible health habits were exchanged for nourishing self-care practices; her despondent disposition was replaced by praise-centric worship. In fact, not only did Hannah choose to mentally surrender her situation, she also agreed to literally surrender the outcome, in this case her future child, to God. Finally Hannah adopted the attitude of surrender that God required of her prior to granting her request for a child. Discover for yourself the extent of Hannah's transformed attitude in her recorded prayer of praise found in 1 Samuel 2. Notice also that Hannah followed through on her commitment to God by selflessly dedicating her son's life to residential internship and a lifetime of service at that temple.

As a result of Hannah's change in attitude, God did not end Hannah's blessings with the birth of Samuel. As a wonderful footnote, Hannah's gratitude and faithfulness were further rewarded by the addition of five more children to her previously childless marriage. Clearly that was beyond anything that Hannah could have ever asked for, thought of, or even whined about!

Real-Time Reflection

From a Waiting-Room perspective, the key lesson that Hannah's experience provides us is that often we must demonstrate a change in our attitude in order for God to facilitate a change in our circumstance. This may require that we too "throw away our whine." Think about your own situation. What are you whining about today? Is it your home, your church, your job, your finances, your kids, your physical weight, or your spiritual wait? Regardless of your situation, God longs to facilitate change in your life. God assures us in Jeremiah 29:11, *"For I **know** the plans I have for you"* (emphasis added). Like Hannah, the duration of your Waiting-Room experience may be dependent on your attitude. Throw away your whine, seek positive encouragement, and offer up a sacrifice of praise, so that you can open God's ears and God's heart to facilitating the blessing He's waiting to fulfill in your life.

Interlude

I'm so glad I've learned to trust Him
Precious Jesus, Saviour, friend
And I know that Thou art with me
Wilt be with me till the end.

Jesus, Jesus how I trust Him
How I've proved Him o'er and o'er
Jesus, Jesus, Precious Jesus
Oh for grace, to trust Him more.

The Waiting Room is designed
to prepare our character and position
our confidence so that we can stand
in the purpose that God has
appointed for us.

Saul: Of Giants and Baggage

**"And the LORD replied, "He is hiding
among the baggage." So they found him
and brought him out, and he stood head
and shoulders above anyone else."
1 Samuel 10:22,23**

suggested reading: 1 Samuel 9-31

Goliath was not the first giant that Saul failed to face
and conquer. Long before he failed to deal with this public
visible giant, Saul had failed to overcome a private emotional giant that became a torment to his entire existence.
As a result, in spite of all the obvious advantages and
resources that Saul had at his disposal, he departed from his
Waiting-Room situation without ever gaining victory over
his personal, debilitating, emotional giant—low self-esteem.

When we are first introduced to Saul, in 1 Samuel 9:1,2,
we discover some interesting things about him. Apparently
Saul came from a "chosen" tribe, an affluent family, and his
father was a man of great influence. Saul clearly had all the
rights, privileges, and entitlements that one could ask for. In
addition to his wealthy and reputable family status, apparently Saul had inherited some great genes. He is described
as being *"the most handsome man in Israel—head and
shoulders above anyone else"* (1 Samuel 9:2). Saul was not
just another face in the crowd. He was a tall, dark, and

handsome face in the crowd. In fact, with all that he seemed to have going for him, socially and physically, Saul (with his distinguished looks and impressive bearing) could be expected to quite literally stand out in any crowd. Oddly enough, this was not the case.

In spite of his many advantages, Saul struggled throughout his life with a common emotional giant—the giant of low self-esteem. We first catch a glimpse of the root of this weakness, when Saul initially met Samuel in 1 Samuel 9:6-27. It is interesting to note that when Saul had a problem, in this case his father's missing donkeys, he neither turned to God nor God's available services through the prophet Samuel. In fact, Saul was poised to proceed to action without first seeking divine assistance. Saul appeared unaware of the existence of Samuel, and it was Saul's *servant* who indicated that such a divine resource might be worth tapping into. The first issue with Saul—and this permeated his life story—was his failure to seek divine assistance. When Saul eventually met Samuel in verse 18, it is clear that he did not recognize the man of God, even as he conversed with him. Clearly Saul's spiritual battery was operating on low. It is disturbing that he could not discern God's messenger as one considers the magnitude of Saul's future leadership role as King of Israel. So beyond the propensity to operate without the benefit of divine assistance, Saul's ability to discern spiritual matters and resources was also somewhat questionable.

Human nature demands that we have something "secure" to place our confidence in. With all Saul's privilege, positioning, and physical advantages, yet his obvious lack of spiritual connection, one would expect that he had a huge dose of self-reliance and confidence. Instead, what Saul seemed to have is a gigantic portion of low self-esteem. Saul's initial response to Samuel, when presented with God's call to lead Israel as king, demonstrates a self-focused, self-absorbed, and selfish delusion regarding his life purpose. Saul frantically pointed out, *"But I'm only from Benjamin, the smallest tribe in Israel, and my family is the least important of all the families of that tribe!"* (1 Samuel 9:21). I would be somewhat comforted if I believed that Saul was deliberately attempting to deceive Samuel. I believe, however, that Saul had actually deceived himself and was speaking from the heart and soul of his delusional insecurity. Saul did not want to be a king. Saul did not want to achieve great things for his people. Saul was content to live an ordinary and easy life within his established family and community rather than be the one on whom a nation pinned its future hopes and dreams. Saul held a warped and unrealistic perspective of his abilities and resources because he had not yet learned to recognize, respect, or respond to God's calling in his life. Saul was trapped by the giant of low self-esteem!

We are not told how long Saul had to wait between Samuel's private anointing and his public appointment as Israel's first king. We do know that his father's missing donkeys were eventually found, his spiritual batteries were temporarily charged (1 Samuel 10:6), and God began to use Saul as His instrument for prophetic messages. The sad truth is, however, that although Saul became God's *instrument*, he never really became God's *servant*. Consequently, Saul never enjoyed the inner peace and confidence that comes from a fully surrendered, purpose-driven life. On the day of Saul's public inauguration, when the entire nation was assembled together to crown their king, insecure Saul was nowhere to be found. (Recognize that this was no small feat for someone who towered head and shoulders above everyone else!) Rather than step up to his God-given appointment, Saul had scurried into hiding. In fact, it was God himself who put an end to Saul's gutless game of hide and seek. When Samuel finally found Saul, he was figuratively curled up in the fetal position, thumb in mouth, cowering among *the baggage*. How childish! How shameful! How unbecoming for the first and future leader of that great nation! It is astonishing and sad to see the grip the giant of low self-esteem had on Saul's life. At the moment that Saul should have exercised his leadership with God-centered confidence, he instead demonstrated humiliating cowardice. Given the rare opportunity to ignite national solidarity and pride, Saul infused his soon-to-be subjects with a spirit of doubt and dissension.

Saul's experience illustrates that the Waiting Room is designed to prepare our character and position our confidence so that we can stand in the purpose that God has appointed for us. Because Saul forfeited his Waiting-Room victory, he spent his lifetime hiding behind emotional baggage. His mental instability and his disastrous personal and familial legacy were self-imposed, avoidable outcomes, resulting from a warped perspective of self and, more importantly, of God. Unfortunately, the giant of low self-esteem triumphed in Saul's life.

Real-Time Reflection

What giant do you face today in your Waiting-Room experience? What character flaw, warped perspective, dysfunctional relationship, or false paradigm do you need to face and conquer? What fears and thoughts are forcing you into hiding behind emotional baggage? God calls you today to stand tall. By standing on His shoulders, you can tower above your giant and gain the victory that you need to confidently face your future. Be assured that as you rely on God and face your giants, He will prepare and position you to fulfill His purpose. Only as a surrendered servant will you be able to confidently and peacefully step into the awesome appointment that He has designed just for you—and that is a destiny worth waiting for!

The faithfulness with which we serve through each of our Waiting-Room appointments may well determine our eligibility for promotion to God's highest calling on our lives.

David: Leadership Fundamentals Part 1

**"But God removed him (Saul) from the
kingship and replaced him with David, a man
about whom God said, 'David son of Jesse
is a man after my own heart, for he will do
everything I want him to.'" Acts 13:22**

suggested reading: 1 Samuel 16-1 Kings 2

David's official enrolment in "leadership studies" began
unexpectedly at the young age of fifteen. It was at that time
that Samuel was led by God to Jesse's household to seek out
the successor to Saul's kingdom. The fact that Jesse presented all his sons except David to Samuel as prospective
candidates for this honour suggests that David was, by all
appearances, a most unlikely candidate. David did not possess the age, experience, or political interests that would
readily qualify him for the leadership role. But God was not
focused on David's current position; He was focused on
David's future potential. God was not deterred by David's
outward appearance; He was captivated by David's heart.
David possessed the one quality that Israel had yet to see in
a royal leader. David had a servant's heart. Whereas Saul
had been an instrument sporadically used by God, David
would be an obedient servant, the only Bible character to
receive the honour *"a man after [God's] own heart"* (Acts
13:22). This servant disposition that David possessed in his

core being was the prerequisite that God required to enrol him in "leadership studies."

Although David was anointed privately by Samuel at age fifteen, it would be another fifteen years, literally another lifetime, before he would actually receive his first public appointment. God knew that David needed the incubation of a significant Waiting-Room period to master his required areas of development. In the Waiting Room, David would acquire the wisdom, experience, and political savvy that would equip him for his future appointment. In addition, his extensive course in "leadership studies" would provide David with hands-on skills in three key leadership development areas: handling promotions, managing problems, and dealing with interpersonal conflict.

Following David's surprise anointing by Samuel, drastic change did not immediately take place in the routine and activities of David's life. For the most part, he went back to his sheep-tending, song-writing, harp-playing lifestyle with no specific transition plan in mind. But a transformation was unfolding for David's life. The Bible states that, *"The Spirit of the LORD came mightily upon him from that day on"* (1 Samuel 16:13).

The first lesson that David had to learn in his leadership-development program was how to deal with promotions. As a shepherd in those days, he basically occupied the lowest rung of the socio-economic ladder. This was particularly a humble beginning for a future king. But even while hanging out with the sheep, David had been developing his musical abilities. Consequently, when a job posting for a palace musician became available, one of his father's servants immediately recommended David as *"a talented harp player"* (1 Samuel 16:18) with precisely the calibre of skill and the consistency of temperament needed to play for the mentally unstable King Saul. It is amazing how God was able to use David's simple yet well-developed hobby to provide a shepherd boy with access and exposure to the royal courts, royal protocol, and royalty. In fact, because of David's skill, disposition and capability, Saul soon invited David to serve as an armour bearer in his court. What an awesome opportunity this provided for David to receive lessons in how to lead (and how not to lead) a nation. From his modest beginnings as a shepherd, David's divinely appointed development plan included promotion to palace musician, armour bearer, commander of the royal army, commander of a dissident army, king of Judah, and finally king of all Israel. Although it was a full twenty-two years between Samuel's anointing and David's appointment as king of the entire nation of Israel, as David was promoted to roles of increasing visibility, complexity, and responsibility, he maintained a servant's heart and attitude as well as a reliance on God.

Real-Time Reflection

Is your Waiting-Room situation taking you into spaces and places that you had not expected to operate within? Are there some environments, roles, or duties that you are being asked to take on that don't quite line up to your original game plan? From David's story we can learn that the Waiting Room may provide us with opportunities for access, exposure, and service in unexpected roles and environments. The faithfulness with which we serve through each of our Waiting-Room appointments may well determine our eligibility for promotion to God's highest calling on our lives. Regardless of the public adulation received, David never wavered in acknowledging the source of his strength and successes. His servant-leadership disposition enabled God to eventually promote him higher and higher until he achieved the highest titles available: "King of Israel" and, more importantly, *a man after [God's] own heart* (Acts 13:22). Now *there* is a promotion worth waiting for!

Our waiting room experience may provide the qualifying experiences and sanctifying ordeals that will strengthen our character, enabling us to handle the triumphs and the troubles that inevitably accompany God's call.

David: Leadership Fundamentals Part 2

**"For when your faith is tested, your endurance
has a chance to grow. So let it grow,
for when your endurance is fully developed,
you will be strong in character and ready
for anything." James 1:3**

suggested reading: 1 Samuel 16-1 Kings 2

Aside from handling promotions, David also learned to deal with problems. Big problems. As a simple shepherd, it may have seemed that life for David was fairly problem free. However, David had to deal with the stigma of his occupation, the ridicule of his brothers, and even the occasional wild animal that would attack his father's sheep. David developed a thick skin that allowed him to deflect negative opinions and stand firm in the face of real and present danger. The secret to David's self-confidence and courage was not found in fancy military training, sophisticated armament, or even physical prowess. When requesting permission to "take out" the giant Goliath, David revealed the source of his assurance as, *"The Lord who saved me from the claws of the lion and the bear"* (1 Samuel 17:37). Because David had experienced God's guidance, strength, and protection with his flock, he was confident about God's ability to assist him in weightier problems—namely the giant, Goliath. Without sword, spear, or javelin but simply in the name of the Lord, David, the shepherd-musician, was able to slay Goliath, something that all Israel's trained soldiers and their qualified (but not sanctified) leader, King Saul, were unable to accomplish. David's leadership studies had taught him a fail-proof method for dealing with problems. Reliance on God's guidance and strength proved to be a key success factor throughout David's leadership life when it came to dealing with problems.

A final lesson that David had to learn in his Waiting-Room development program was how to successfully deal with interpersonal conflict. Apparently David was born into a family in which he was last and somewhat least. Likely his apparent contentment with spending his days alone shepherding and making music were not deemed the most ambitious or manly of pursuits! Also the fact that David's brothers were all in the military (1 Samuel 17:19) and were involved in important matters of national security further added to the lack of credibility of David's opinions or perspectives. We can only imagine then, when it was *David* who was anointed as a future king, and *David* who offered to get rid of Goliath, that his brothers were filled with contempt, jealousy, and ridicule for their misguided youngest sibling.

- Through his interaction with his brothers, David learned to defend himself verbally. (Ultimately David was also learning other important leadership skills.)

- Through his interaction with wild animals and the giant, Goliath, David learned to defend himself physically.

- Through his conflict with Saul, David learned to protect himself physically, while setting an example for respectful service.

- Through his friendship with Jonathan, David learned to commit himself to another emotionally.

- Through the Saul-and-Jonathan-relationship dynamic, David experienced the very best and very worst of human nature.

Ultimately, the contempt of David's brothers paled in comparison to the insane jealousy and murderous hatred that Saul felt toward David. Thankfully, David had learned, through his dealings with his brothers, not to take things too personally. He had learned to wait on the Lord, and this ensured and secured his place in history as a man after God's own heart and a respected king of Israel.

There is an additional sub-plot in David's life worth mentioning. It is important to recognize that if anyone in David's life had a right to be jealous and hateful, it would have been his best friend, Jonathan. As Saul's son, Jonathan was the natural and rightful heir-successor to the throne. Seeing David's growing popularity and proximity to national and political issues, Jonathan could well have deduced that David was a threat to his own future prospects and chosen to be an accomplice to his father's various murder plots. Jonathan, however, must have perceived David's heart. The friendship that formed between the two in spite of the many obvious reasons for distrust is as unlikely as it is exemplary.

Handling promotions, addressing problems, and dealing with interpersonal conflict were all leadership skills that David was taught through his fifteen-year Waiting-Room period. When David was finally publicly appointed as king, he had a track record of faithfulness, service, leadership, acumen, and courage that made him undisputedly eligible for national leadership responsibilities. Perhaps more remarkably, throughout his development, David maintained a servant's heart and a reliance on God. Though David did not achieve character perfection, he certainly demonstrated character completion in the way he chose to handle his future successes and failures. Unlike Saul his predecessor, not only was David obviously *qualified* for the role, his leadership was also *sanctified* by his close friendship with God. Truly he became "a man after God's own heart."

David's life is a testament to the value of time well spent in the Waiting Room. The period between God's call on our life and assuming the responsibilities of that call may seem tedious, purposeless, and wasteful when viewed through our human perception. The reality is that our Waiting-Room experience may provide the qualifying experiences and sanctifying ordeals that will strengthen our character, enabling us to handle the triumphs and the troubles that inevitably accompany God's call. As James assures us, *"when your endurance is fully developed, you will be strong in character and ready for anything"* (James 1:4). David's adult life demonstrated that he possessed the strength of character needed to exhibit grace under fire, repentance following error, and respect in the face of ignorance.

Real-Time Reflection

Evaluate your Waiting-Room experience today. What attitudes and qualities are you developing? What people, problems, and promotions are dealing with? What's the nature of your spiritual connection and reliance on God? You may not be called to slay a giant or lead a nation. But God longs to call you a child after His own heart. Commit today to developing a servant's heart—obedient, loyal, and reliant on your Master. Then, like David, you will grow *strong in character and ready for anything* (James 1:4). That will make the waiting worthwhile!

Our Waiting-Room experience
can provide a clarifying revelation
about the spiritual mindset and
motivation of the people closest to us.

Job: Close Encounters of the Revealing Kind

⌒ ⟶ ⟶ ⟶ ⌒ ⌒

**"When Job prayed for his friends,
the LORD restored his fortunes."
Job 42:10**

suggested reading: Job 1-42

When we are first introduced to Job in Job chapter 1, we meet a man who has, for all intents and purposes, "arrived." Whether viewed from the perspective of physical health, material wealth, leadership breadth, or spiritual depth, Job had it going on. Job had earned an enviable reputation as *"blameless...a man of complete integrity...[who] feared God and stayed away from evil"* (Job 1:1). By all appearances, not only had Job's ship come in, it had docked, dropped anchor, and unloaded some pretty impressive cargo!

So when the well-established, integrity-filled, spirit-centered Job was unexpectedly ushered into a series of the most horrific Waiting-Room conditions possible, undoubtedly everyone, including Job, was astonished by the sudden reversal of fortune. Within what seemed to be a disturbingly concentrated period of time, Job's legacy, wealth, and health were stripped away, reducing him, quite literally, to nothing but inconsolable grief, blistered skin, and aching bones. But the secret to Job's steadfast faithfulness while he endured the pain, shame, and blame of his Waiting-Room experience came from his understanding that *reversal of fortune does not signify a reversal of God's favour*. Job maintained the spiritual discernment to confidently assert *"The LORD gave, and the LORD hath taken away; blessed be the name of the LORD"* (Job 1:21 KJV). God Himself was able to say of Job, *"There is no one on earth like him; he is blameless and upright, a man who fears God and shuns evil"* (Job 2:3 NIV). Throughout his pain- and grief-filled Waiting-Room circumstances, Job consistently displayed a remarkable degree of spiritual integrity. Although he never claimed to know the reason for his situation, what Job did know was his God.

Interestingly enough, Job's character was not the only one challenged by his devastating losses. I have always found it ironic that Job's wife was the only one of Job's immediate family members who survived the natural disasters that claimed the lives of all of their ten children. I suspect that as wide as the magnitude of Job's personal losses were, having a bitter, grief-stricken, doubt-filled wife rattling off irrational suggestions in his boil-infested ears added a fresh, salty sting to Job's emotional wounds. I suspect that Job's wife caused him more grief through her disgust with life than she would have through her untimely death. Regardless of my suspicions, I am somewhat empathetic to this woman's situation. After all, Job was not the only loser in this scenario. Here is a woman who had lost her children—her source of value; her wealth—her source of security; and seemed poised to lose her husband—her source of physical and spiritual companionship. It really is no wonder then that Mrs. Job temporarily lost her mind and misguidedly encouraged her spirit-centered husband to *"curse God and die"* (Job 2:9). That Job's character had remained unchanged by his Waiting-Room horrors is evident in his insightful yet tactful response to his grieving wife: *"'You talk like a god-less woman. Should we accept only good things from the hand of God and never anything bad?' So in all this, Job said nothing wrong"* (Job 2:10). Clearly Job's faith had not been moved by his involuntary foray into the Waiting Room. The Waiting Room had, however, done much to reveal the spiritual vulnerability of Job's wife.

Shortly after Mrs. Job was exposed for her shortcomings, another "reveal" awaits the suffering Job. This time, "encouragement" arrives in the form of three of Job's closest friends and spiritual confidants. Undoubtedly, these were men who had previously shared values, religious philosophies, and spiritual principles with the spirit-centered Job. This is evident by the fact that when they arrived they honoured the Jewish tradition of remaining silent in the presence of a mourner until that mourner finally speaks. For seven days, they kept their mouths shut and comforted Job merely through the gift of their presence. Perhaps if they left immediately after that, they would have avoided challenging Job's spiritual integrity and thereby incurring the anger of God. But when, after seven long days, Job finally broke the code of silence, all the pent-up speculations, accusations, and condemnations that his good friends had withheld came spilling out. Chapter after chapter of profound-but-misguided theological monologues were provided by Job's well-intentioned friends. Not only was Job accused by his spiritual mentors of suffering because of unconfessed sin in his life, he was also reprimanded for his stubborn refusal to admit that he was wrong, in order to end his current and future suffering. As the saying goes, with friends like those, Job did not need enemies! Not only did Job have to contend with excruciating physical pain and tremendous emotional grief due to his great personal losses, but he also had to endure an unwarranted spiritual lynching from his most trusted companions. In the final analysis, it is God, and not Job, who ultimately set the record straight for Job's friends. Not only were they dead wrong about Job's character, they were deadly wrong about the character of God.

Fortunately, Job's Waiting-Room traumas did nothing to compromise the integrity of his character. What the Waiting Room did reveal was the true characters of those closest to Job, those who he had assumed shared his values, beliefs, and spiritual perspectives about the wisdom, love, and benevolence of God. While we may remain unchanged, often our own Waiting-Room experience can provide a clarifying revelation about the spiritual mindset and motivation of the people closest to us. We can take a lesson from the life of Job in that, *"when...[he] prayed for his friends, the Lord restored his fortunes"* (Job 42:10). With the intercessory prayer of Job ringing in their ears, Job's friends repented. More importantly, Job's own healing occurred and he was restored to twice his former wealth, rigorous health, and renewed family status.

Real-Time Reflection

As you reside in your Waiting Room today, take a good look around at those who you consider close to you. Pay particular attention to those who are choosing to spend time with you and those who seem to have forgotten your phone number. Listen closely to the type of "encouragement" that you are getting from your friends and mentors who do show up. Pray for the discernment to accept spirit-centered advice and the courage to reject misguided opinions. Keep in mind that even well-intentioned friends may provide you with very bad advice. Above all, even while you wait, remember to pray for all those who God has placed within your life. Not only may your prayer be the catalyst that influences positive change in their lives, your prayer may well hold the key that unlocks the door to your own restoration. So why not bow right now to begin this prayer process? Your restoration is on its way. What are you waiting for?

Faithful service
in the Waiting Room
pleases God.

Jesus: A Saviour Waits

**"I must be about my Father's
business." Luke 2:49 KJV**

suggested reading: Luke 1-3:22

The last person I would expect to run into in the
Waiting Room would be Jesus. Let's be real; if ever someone
was born with an impressive title and a clear job descrip-
tion, this was the man! Talk about role clarity and a sense
of purpose, the one called *Immanuel*—literally *God with
us*—was crystal clear about what He had to accomplish
while He was here on Earth.

At just twelve years of age, as He taught religious leaders
in the temple, Jesus let His parents know that He was clear
about His mission. When He stated that He *"must be
about...[His] Father's business"* (Luke 2:49 KJV), rest
assured He was not handing out coupons to promote
Joseph's carpenter shop! And yet Jesus' official ministry did
not commence until He was thirty years of age. Now ordi-
narily, I wouldn't get too terribly fussed about someone "getting it together" at age thirty. But this was not an ordinary
circumstance! Jesus did not have the seventy-plus-year
lifespan that we typically enjoy today. Let's do the math: at

twelve, Jesus knew His mission; at thirty, He began His mission; and by thirty-three, He was dead—mission accomplished. Hello? That means that at least eighteen years of our Saviour's life were spent in the Waiting Room, anticipating His Father's call to action. Follow me closely: over 55 percent of our Saviour's life was spent—in...the...Waiting...Room! Does that make sense to you? Truly, God's thoughts are not our thoughts and His ways are not our ways (see Isaiah 55:8)—because I just don't get it!

So if the One who was charged with the ultimate, divinely-appointed mission of saving humanity spent 90 percent of his time on Earth doing "ordinary things" and at least 55 percent of His time in the Waiting Room with a clear understanding of His calling, why do *we* grumble, complain, and lose faith when we have to endure Waiting-Room circumstances, even for a moment? Apparently we need to understand that our wait is not a waste, as long as God waits with us. E. G. White, in her classic, *The Desire of Ages*, shares an interesting perspective on the waiting years of Jesus' life. She states:

> *[Jesus] lived to please, honor and glorify His Father in the common things of life. His work began in consecrating the lowly trade of the craftsmen who toil for their daily bread. He was doing God's service just as much when labouring at the carpenter's bench as when working miracles for the multitude.*[2]

Hold on, let's read that again, "*He was doing God's service just as much when labouring at the carpenter's bench as*

[2] Ellen G. White, *The Desire of Ages* (Oshawa: Pacific Press Publishing Association, 1940) p. 74.

when working miracles for the multitude" Quick—grab your *Webster's* and look up the word *wait. To wait* literally means "to serve; to hold oneself ready for an arrival or occurrence; to be in expectation of something." No resting on His laurels, bemoaning His sorry state for our Saviour. Jesus was preparing and positioning Himself in anticipation through the entire eighteen years—literally *waiting*—and it is at the end of *that* waiting period God was able to say, *"This is my beloved Son, in whom I am well pleased"* (Matthew 3:17 KJV). Now, I do not mean to be rude but, what on earth was God so pleased about? Not one blind man had regained sight, not one leper had been cleansed, and not one dead man had been raised, but God stated He was not just pleased, but *well* pleased! As we read between the lines, it would appear that God was pleased with His Son's service—in the Waiting Room! Let's learn this lesson really well: faithful service in the Waiting Room pleases God.

Real-Time Reflection

I'm not sure what it is you feel God has called you to do. I don't know what great purpose you have determined you need to fulfill. What I am pretty sure of is that, however important your task might seem to you, it doesn't begin to compare with saving the entire world from sin. So what have you decided to do while you hang out in the Waiting Room? How have you decided to serve and, consequently, please your Heavenly Father? No matter how common, insignificant, or unfruitful your present efforts may seem, know that God is expecting faithful service. If the Waiting Room was good enough for Jesus, perhaps it's an okay place for us to spend some time. Hmmm...something to think about.

Frankly, if I ever get to hear that God is even a little pleased with me, it won't matter how much Waiting-Room time I had to endure. At the end of the day, God's *"Well done"* is the only thing that really matters anyway. Now *that*, fellow wait'er, is something truly worth waiting for!

Satisfactory resolution to Waiting-Room
issues occurs when we transfer our
faith from human inventions
to divine intervention.

The Woman With the Issue of Blood: One Woman's Issues

"Daughter, your faith has made you well. Go in peace. You have been healed." Mark 5:34

suggested reading: Mark 5:21-34

If ever there was a character who experienced the painful side of the Waiting Room, the New Testament woman with the issue of blood was one. Although we never learn her actual name, her legacy illustrates the relationship between active faith and divine healing and provides guidance and encouragement to those of us who have to wait under the most unfavourable conditions.

Talk about a woman with issues! We often dwell on the fact that this woman had suffered for twelve long and painful years with *"an issue of blood"* (Mark 5:25 KJV) Bible scholars describe her disease as a chronic menstrual or uterine hemorrhage disorder that seemed incurable. That condition in itself would have been a tremendous issue. Experiencing "that time of the month" every day of the month for twelve long years? Pardon the pun, but that must have been a real drain! The interesting thing about her particular disease is that, although it was largely a very private disorder, its symptoms caused the patient to be exposed to very public consequences.

In the first place, she was a woman, and a menstruating one at that, within a cultural and religious regime that considered such women to be ritually unclean and consequently not able to mingle in social settings. Social isolation was therefore an issue that the woman would have been subjected to for twelve lonely years. To violate that custom would undoubtedly have had more humiliating and perhaps deadly consequences than to quietly live her diseased life on the margins of the community. (Recall the punishment warranted by the woman caught in adultery.) To make matters worse, an issue that further contributed to the woman's social isolation would have been her gender. As a woman seemingly single and alone in a patriarchal culture where women were considered second-class citizens, there is no evidence of a male figure in her life who could champion her case, seek medical expertise, or even provide financial support to assist her. Clearly, social isolation was a pervasive issue in this woman's life.

Another issue that the woman appeared to have had was financial hardship. Mark outlines her predicament when he states, *"She had suffered a great deal from many doctors through the years and had spent everything she had to pay them, but she had gotten no better"* (Mark 5:26). Although this is evidence of the woman's admirable persistence, bravery, and willingness to trade her limited wealth for health, it would appear that her investment had not paid off. Mark goes on to say, *"In fact, she was worse."* I believe that *worse* refers not only to her actual physical suffering but to her financial status as a result of those apparently painful, possibly humiliating, and clearly unsuccessful medical interventions. We can conclude that financial pressures exacerbated the physical stress for this deeply afflicted woman.

Beyond the social, financial, and physical issues that plagued the woman, there must have been some deep-seated emotional issues that also kept her mind and spirit in a state of turmoil. Possible hormonal imbalances coupled with the anemic state of her constantly hemorrhaging body would likely have made her a candidate for a mental ward. Depression, irritability, moodiness, low self-esteem: all those qualities that we attribute to premenstrual syndrome may well have been constant companions of this woman. In addition, there would have been the spiritual distress caused by her alienation from the religious community and her permanent state of "uncleanness." Such emotional and spiritual issues were enough to keep the woman separated from her family, church, community, and, ultimately, her God—the very elements that could have brought peace, comfort, and support to her ailing existence. So to say that this woman had an issue of blood is to grossly understate the magnitude of her devastating situation. Physical, social, financial, and emotional issues were draining this woman's very existence.

With so many issues conspiring against her, and with a twelve-year Waiting-Room stay to her claim, this woman would have been the last person we would expect to see reaching out for Jesus. What I find awesome and inspiring from a Waiting-Room perspective is that, as this woman's issues became more pronounced, apparently so did her faith in God. As her situation became more desperate, so did her need for God. And as her public humiliation and isolation deepened, so apparently did her private commitment and connectivity to God. What resulted was a transfer of this woman's persistence, bravery, and faith from the human to the Divine. Only when that transfer occurred, as symbolized through her legendary touch on the hem of Jesus' robe, could her complete healing take place. Jesus commended this woman's faith in Him and restored her in ways that the medical system could never have done. Not only did He speak healing to her body—which would ultimately resolve her physical, social, and financial issues—but He also pronounced peace on her soul, addressing her deep-seated emotional and spiritual turmoil. That outcome exceeded any that the woman could have ever hoped, prayed, or paid for. In a single statement from her Lord, all her issues were addressed! That outcome was likely worth the wait.

Real-Time Reflection

Does your Waiting-Room experience seem overwhelming because of the depth and breadth of your issues? Are you trusting your outcomes to proven solutions and human strategies? If so, the story of the woman with the issues reminds us that satisfactory resolution to Waiting-Room issues occurs when we transfer our faith from human inventions to divine intervention. Perhaps it is time that we rethink our Waiting-Room paradigm. Perhaps it is not a matter of us waiting on God to deliver us. Perhaps God has been the One patiently waiting on us to stop focusing on the size of our issues and to start focusing on the limitlessness of His solutions. Hmmm...now there's something worth thinking about even while we wait!

Our role in the Waiting Room
is not to seek human insight
but to pray for spiritual foresight.

The Man Born Blind:
The Delusion of Sight

**"He was born blind so the power
of God could be seen in Him."
John 9:3**

suggested reading: John 9:1-34

Having never lost my eyesight, I really cannot say that I know how the man Jesus healed in John 9 felt. What we are told is that this man was blind from birth. He had never known the beauty of a sunset, experienced the smile of a toddler, or recoiled at the look of reprimand from a parent. In fact, it would appear that this man had no real claim to fame other than being known as a *"blind beggar"* (John 9:8). His physical and financial conditions defined his identity within the community; the rest of his character seemed to have little impact on his societal value. We are not told at what age this man encountered Jesus, but we can deduce that he was old enough to be called a "man," dependent enough to be known as a "beggar," and blind enough to be easily identifiable by his handicap. Regardless of his exact age, he had literally spent his lifetime in a dark and desolate Waiting Room.

Jesus' disciples, adhering to the indoctrinated beliefs of the Jewish culture, attempted to demonstrate their deep theological knowledge by striking up a conversation with their leader. *"Teacher...why was this man born blind?"* (John 9:2). Not even waiting for Jesus' response, they rhetorically queried, *"Was it a result of his own sins or those of his parents?"* Like many of us today, the disciples believed that the man's condition was explainable from a human perspective. Clearly the man's tragic fate was either the result of his own poor choices, in which case, shame on him, or his parents' bad decisions, in which case, blame could be placed on them. After all, couldn't all personal tragedies be explained by the shame or blame of someone?

Jesus wasted no time in dispelling this long-standing myth. He quickly corrected his disciples' arrogant thinking by asserting that, at least in this particular case, their rationale was inaccurate. He stated, the man had been *"born blind so the power of God could be seen in Him"* (John 9:3). He then proceeded to create a saliva mix, paste it on the blind man's eyes, provide him with washing instructions, and, ultimately, facilitate his complete healing. It is interesting to note that Jesus never required that the man do anything that was beyond his physical or financial means. Although the man could not see, he could *listen* to the words and *follow* the instructions of the divine teacher. As a result, beyond sight, Jesus was able to give the blind beggar a much-needed gift of dignity by allowing him to participate in his own healing.

It is then that the issue of true blindness became somewhat murky. Some members of the formerly blind beggar's community were unable to "see" him as a healthy, fully functioning, contributing, sight-filled man. His period of waiting had ended. His lifelong deficiency had been restored. As Jesus predicted, the glory of the Lord had been revealed in such a profound and miraculous way that the man's healing could only be attributed to the Master's touch. That is, if people chose to "see" the evidence before their very eyes.

This short yet profound story provides a couple of Waiting-Room reflections worth paying attention to. In the first place, we need to be careful not to use our Waiting-Room predicament to justify clinging to personal shame or to rationalize assigning unsubstantiated blame. The simple fact is that often we will not know why God is allowing certain events to happen in our lives or the lives of others. Our role in the Waiting Room is not to seek human insight but to pray for spiritual foresight that sees beyond our current situation and focuses instead on God's greater plan for our lives. The second Waiting-Room reflection that the blind beggar's healing brings to light is the fact that there will always be those who refuse to "see" the transformation that God has performed in our character, situation, or lives. We need to ensure that we never let the blindness of others block us from seeing and claiming *"the power of God"* in our lives.

Real-Time Reflection

If today you find yourself in a Waiting-Room situation, let the blind beggar man provide a blueprint for you. Even though you cannot *see* your future, you can choose to *listen to* and to *follow* God's leading in your life. You can choose to partner with Him in facilitating your deliverance. And when your situation has improved, you can share with those around you how *"the power of God"* has transformed your life. Whether they choose to acknowledge God's power or not will depend on whether they see through the eyes of human insight or the perspective of spiritual foresight.

God's timing allows Him to display His awesome glory to and through us in miraculous ways.

Mary, Martha and Lazarus: A Deadly Test of Friendship

"Jesus responded, 'Didn't I tell you that you will see God's glory if you believe?'" John 11:40

suggested reading: John 11:1-45

There is nothing as traumatic as the spiritual isolation we sometimes feel in our Waiting-Room situations. Although we know intuitively that others have shared, are sharing, or will one day share our experience, that thought provides little comfort when our time of waiting comes.

Mary, Martha, and Lazarus were very close to Jesus. The disciples may have been Jesus' followers, but these three were considered His friends. When our Saviour needed a place to relax, this sibling group was more than happy to welcome Him into their home. So it really seems curious that when Lazarus became ill and Jesus was called, He did not respond immediately. It wasn't as if their message lacked clarity: *"Lord, the one you love is very sick"* (John 11:3). Nor does it seem that Jesus had other pressing matters to attend to. John makes it crystal clear: *"Although Jesus loved Martha, Mary, and Lazarus, He stayed where He was for the next two days and did not go to them"* (John 11:5,6). Ouch! That must have hurt. Death was knocking down their door, and their dear and, more importantly, powerful friend seemed to be loafing.

Thankfully, the family was not left without a promise. Jesus assured those around Him that, *"Lazarus's sickness will not end in death...it is for glory of God"* (John 11:4). So the agonizing wait for promise fulfillment began. Have you ever waited by the bedside of someone who was sick or dying? A deathbed is typically not the type of place that most people voluntarily gravitate towards. I can only begin to imagine the excruciating burden of hopelessness and helplessness that Mary and Martha felt, knowing that as their brother lay dying, the One whom they loved had chosen to stay away. The One who had brought healing and deliverance to total and sometimes ungrateful strangers now seemed to neglect His closest friends.

But God had a much bigger plan—way beyond this family's needs. It would take a couple of days, two to be exact, but Jesus' timing was impeccable. E. G. White writes:

> *Christ had not only the loved ones at Bethany to think of; He had the training of His disciples to consider. They were to be His representatives to the world that the Father's blessing might embrace all. For their sake He permitted Lazarus to die. Had He restored him from illness to health, the miracle that is the most positive evidence of His divine character would not have been performed...In delaying to come to Lazarus, Christ had a purpose of mercy toward those who had not received Him. He tarried that by raising Lazarus from the dead He might give to His stubborn, unbe-*

---

3 Ellen G. White, *The Desire of Ages* (Oshawa: Pacific Press Publishing Association) pp. 528-529.

lieving people...evidence that He was indeed 'the resurrection and the life.' [3]

Even as His friends were trapped despairing in their Waiting Room, God was preparing an award-worthy dramatic display of deliverance—and Lazarus was the unlikely star of the show.

The rest is truly *His*tory. Through the raising of Lazarus, a most powerful Waiting-Room lesson emerges. While healing Lazarus would have generated some public interest, raising him from the dead was worthy of a front-page headline! The testimony this scene provided to God's power and capability had never before been so dramatically witnessed on Earth and provided assurance to believers from that day onward that a resurrection was not only possible, but guaranteed. This Waiting-Room experience assures us that there are occasions when God's timing allows Him to display His awesome glory to and through us in miraculous ways.

Real-Time Reflection

If you are confident of God's promises and leading in your life and are patiently waiting to see the fulfillment, learn a lesson from Mary, Martha, and Lazarus' experience and chill out! God may be getting ready to call you forward into a miraculously *renewed* life. The waiting will eventually be over and, who knows, you may just see God's glory if you believe!

Focusing our energy on matters
of pride and prominence will never
position us for success within or
beyond the Waiting Room.

The Disciples: How Not to Wait

**"'Why are you sleeping?' he
[Jesus] asked. 'Get up and pray.
Otherwise temptation will
overpower you.'" Luke 22:46**

suggested reading: Luke 22

Prior to Jesus' crucifixion, it was clear that the disciples just didn't "get" the whole Christianity thing. Yes, they were growing and beginning to develop the skills and attributes that they would require to continue on after their teacher left them. But they had yet to develop the much-needed faith, love, and commitment that would take them beyond their self-centredness, equipping them to work wholeheartedly on spreading the gospel of Christ.

Luke 22 provides a revealing and pathetic look at the lack of spiritual maturity that the disciples possessed, even as the final, critical hours of Christ's ministry approached. Starting with Judas' betrayal arrangements, uncompromised loyalty was clearly an issue for the disciples. Even the sincere Peter, who swore his undying commitment to his Master, proved to be sincerely wrong when put to the loyalty test. Although the disciples had spent three years in the presence of the Divine, they were still enslaved by their very human dispositions.

During the observance of what should have been a reverent and sobering Last Supper, the disciples found themselves arguing like children in a schoolyard over who would be the greatest in the kingdom. Ironically, it did not occur to any of them that they would not have to worry about *positions* in the kingdom if they didn't adopt the necessary attitudes to obtain *citizenship* there! Rather than trying to gain the last bits of wisdom and attempting to serve and encourage their departing Lord, the disciples remained self-absorbed and obsessed with matters of pride, position, and prominence, which, though important from a human perspective, were irrelevant in the eyes of the Divine.

Perhaps the most compelling evidence of the disciples' spiritual immaturity, however, is found on the Mount of Olives in the Garden of Gethsemane. What an honour to be called by the soon-to-be Saviour of the world to this momentous Waiting-Room experience! What a disappointment that the disciples failed to recognize their sacred appointment as supporters of Earth's Saviour. Tragically, during the most spiritually, physically, and emotionally tumultuous hours of Jesus' life on Earth, when He really needed and requested friends who He could lean on, the disciples fell asleep. Asleep! Luke 22:45 explains that the disciples were *"exhausted from grief."* The same verse in the Clear Word says they were *"exhausted from worry."* Worry, grief, cares of life, concern about their futures—these were the issues that were draining the disciples' strength, clouding their reasoning, and stealing their ability to support and encourage their beloved teacher and friend. Characteristically, even in his darkest moment, Jesus expressed concern not for Himself but for His misguided companions. He actually commanded them to *"Get up and pray"* (Luke 22:46). Our selfless Saviour was not as concerned about His own well-being but about the spiritual strength the disciples would undoubtedly require to successfully face the temptations that lay ahead for them. Even as He spoke, the Waiting-Room door was swinging open, and that opportunity for preparation through prayer was forever lost.

Real-Time Reflection

None of us know how or when our Waiting-Room experience will end. Even at this moment, our situation may be on the verge of positive or negative change. From the disciples' experience, however, we can gain valuable insight into how *not* to wait. Focusing our energy on matters of pride and prominence will never position us for success within or beyond the Waiting Room. We can strengthen ourselves spiritually only by disciplining ourselves to *"get up and pray,"* even when that is the last thing we feel we need to or are able to do. The same instruction that a concerned Jesus gave to His disciples in Gethsemane's Waiting-Room drama is the same instruction He provides to us today. Now is not the time to be overwhelmed by stress, grief, and worry. Now is the perfect time to get up, shake off our cares, and begin to pray!

A glorious future awaits us beyond
the tumultuous Waiting Room
of our earthly existence.

All Creation Waits

**"For all creation is waiting eagerly
for that future day when God will
reveal who his children really are."
Romans 8:19**

suggested reading: Romans 8; John 3:16,17

The preceding stories demonstrate clearly how, down through the ages, God has provided individuals with Waiting-Room experiences. We have learned about promises broken and promises fulfilled, healing obtained and healing forfeited, relationships severed and relationships restored, destinies eroded and destinies established. We have observed a wide variety of outcomes, depending on the Waiting-Room choices that each character made.

Incidentally, the Waiting-Room experience has not been relegated to a few select Biblical characters. As Romans 8 assures us, all creation is residing in a figurative Waiting Room, eagerly anticipating that future day when God will reveal who His children really are (Romans 8:19). Why is all creation in a perpetual state of waiting? We need simply to look around us and the answer becomes clear. At the core of our being, all creation longs to be liberated from the inescapable impacts of evil: sickness, poverty, war, separation, conflict, terrorism, and death. All creation groans to be permanently *"released from pain and suffering"* (Romans 8:23).

Beloved, whether you consider yourself to be incubated or trapped within a personal Waiting-Room situation or are languishing in the relative peace and comfort of a more fulfilling domain, as a member of the *"all creation"* family, something deep within you *"groans."* Inevitably you will one day peek between the kitchen blinds, glance at a newspaper headline, flip past a World Vision advertisement, or respond to a frantic phone call and be reminded that our souls are all connected within a universal Waiting-Room situation.

There is, however, no need for despair! Through Romans 8, Paul assures us that help is on the way. A glorious future awaits us beyond the tumultuous Waiting Room of our earthly existence. John 3:16 assures us that our freedom from death and decay has been purchased and paid for through the blood of Christ, and by accepting His sacrifice, our Heavenly citizenship and permanent residency is assured. Paul's letter in Romans 8 instructs us to *"wait patiently and confidently,"* empower ourselves through the Holy Spirit, and trust that all things—including our personal Waiting-Room situations—are working together for our good (Romans 8:26-28).

Real-Time Reflection

If we can learn to wait—God will give us *"new strength"* allowing us to *"fly high on wings like eagles,"* and to run and walk without growing tired (Isaiah 40:31). If we can learn to wait—God will cause *"everything to work together for [our] good"* (Romans 8:28). If we can learn to wait—*"God will give us our full rights as His children"* (Romans 8:23).

When viewed through the eyes of eternity, I am confident that we will all agree our collective Waiting-Room experience was for our good. And *that* reflection, my friends, will be one worth waiting for!

Your Waiting-Room Reflections

**"But those who wait on the LORD will find
new strength. They will fly high on wings like
eagles. They will run and not grow weary.
They will walk and not faint." Isaiah 40:31**

I trust you will agree with me that it has been fascinating reading about and reflecting on the diverse Waiting-Room experiences of these Bible-time characters. I hope also that you will see how the examples from their lives can provide practical tips for encouraging us through our real-time Waiting-Room situations.

My experience as a consultant has taught me that the deepest learning occurs, however, when we can personalize our reflections to our own experiences. The blank lines that follow do not represent a typo. They have been intentionally provided for you to record your own Waiting-Room experiences. Maybe it is an incident from your past or perhaps a very current situation. Hopefully by now, with the added perspective of these Biblical reflections, you recognize your own Waiting-Room episodes. Once you have completed an entry, prayerfully ask God to strengthen your current and future Waiting-Room visits even as you thank Him for how He has guided you through your past stopovers. If you really want to solidify your learning, share your entry with a friend. Find someone who is wrestling with their own Waiting-Room situation and encourage them with reflections of God's fulfillment and deliverance in your own life.

Author's Footnote

Incidentally, I too need ongoing Waiting-Room encouragement. When you have completed your story, I would be thrilled if you would forward me a copy so that I can know for sure that these reflections helped you. In fact, with your permission, I can ensure that many others are strengthened through your personal story. Your reflection can be forwarded to thewaitingroom@rogers.com

The prospect of creating a community of successful "waiters" excites me. The opportunity to continue encouraging others through your stories makes the writing of this book worthwhile. I look forward to hearing your personal story. Please don't keep me waiting!

Summary Reflections
from The Waiting Room

❧ Your Waiting-Room experience may not be about you!

❧ God's timing may be different than our human understanding, but it is always right.

❧ God's delay is never an open invitation to formulate and implement a do-it-yourself plan.

❧ Doing wrong things to achieve right outcomes is not an acceptable way to escape our Waiting Room.

❧ Our Waiting Room may place us at all-time lows so that God can prepare us for all-time highs.

❧ While you are waiting, God may be shaping your deliverance.

❧ Though the circumstance of our waiting may be an ordeal, God's reward for the faithful will be ideal.

❧ Our best choices often involve waiting contentedly on God's leading, anticipating His deliverance, and ultimately celebrating His restoration in our lives.

ᢞ Often we must demonstrate a change in our attitude in order for God to facilitate a change in our circumstance.

ᢞ The Waiting Room is designed to prepare our character and position our confidence so that we can stand in the purpose that God has appointed for us.

ᢞ The faithfulness with which we serve through each of our Waiting-Room appointments may well determine our eligibility for promotion to God's highest calling on our lives.

ᢞ Our Waiting-Room experience may provide the qualifying experiences and sanctifying ordeals that will strengthen our characters, enabling us to handle the triumphs and the troubles that inevitably accompany God's call.

ᢞ Our Waiting-Room experience may provide a clarifying revelation about the spiritual mindset and motivation of the people closest to us.

ᢞ Faithful service in the Waiting Room pleases God.

ᢞ Satisfactory resolution to Waiting-Room issues occurs when we transfer our faith from human inventions to divine interventions.

ᢞ We best resolve Waiting-Room issues by transferring our faith beyond human perceptions and expert inventions to active pursuit of divine intervention.

ᢞ Our role in the Waiting Room is not to seek human insight but to pray for spiritual foresight.

ᢞ God's timing allows Him to display His awesome glory to and through us in miraculous ways.

❧ Focusing our energy on matters of pride and prominence will never position us for success within the waiting or beyond the Waiting Room.

❧ A glorious future awaits us beyond the tumultuous Waiting Room of our earthly existence.